Cut, Color, Trace &

Rebus Stories

38 "Fold-It" Predictable Rebus Stories that Combine Reading and Fine Motor Skills

by
Sherrill B. Flora

illustrated by
Julie Anderson

Key Education
An imprint of Carson-Dellosa Publishing LLC
Greensboro, North Carolina
www.keyeducationpublishing.com

CONGRATULATIONS ON YOUR PURCHASE OF A KEY EDUCATION PRODUCT!

The editors at Key Education are former teachers who bring experience, enthusiasm, and quality to each and every product. Thousands of teachers have looked to the staff at Key Education for new and innovative resources to make their work more enjoyable and rewarding. We are committed to developing educational materials that will assist teachers in building a strong and developmentally appropriate curriculum for young children.

PLAN FOR GREAT TEACHING EXPERIENCES WHEN YOU USE EDUCATIONAL MATERIALS FROM KEY EDUCATION PUBLISHING COMPANY, LLC

Credits
Author: Sherrill B. Flora
Inside Illustrations: Julie Anderson
Editors: Claude Chalk & Karen Seberg
Page Design & Layout: Key Education Staff
Cover Design & Production: Annette Hollister-Papp

Key Education
An imprint of Carson-Dellosa Publishing LLC
PO Box 35665
Greensboro, NC 27425 USA
www.keyeducationpublishing.com

Copyright Notice
© 2012, Carson-Dellosa Publishing LLC. The purchase of this material entitles the buyer to reproduce worksheets and activities for classroom use only—not for commercial resale. Reproduction of these materials for an entire school or district is prohibited. No part of this book may be reproduced (except as noted above), stored in a retrieval system, or transmitted in any form or by any means (mechanically, electronically, recording, etc.) without the prior written consent of Carson-Dellosa Publishing LLC. Key Education is an imprint of Carson-Dellosa Publishing LLC.

Printed in the USA • All rights reserved.

ISBN 978-1-60268-119-4
1-335118091

INTRODUCTION

Cut, Color, Trace & Paste Rebus Stories introduces 50 essential sight words combined with the creative fun of making 38 "Fold-It" rebus story books. Each story uses a multisensory approach as the children trace the new sight words, color and cut out the rebus pictures, glue the pictures in the correct locations, and finally use the rebus visual clues as they read the text aloud. Children are using their auditory, visual, and tactile senses as they build and strengthen their reading and fine motor skills.

Rebus stories are not only great for beginning readers, but they can also boost the skills and confidence of struggling readers. Even those students who are not able to recognize any sight words yet, can follow along and "read" using the pictures to tell the predictable story.

Cut, Color, Trace & Paste Rebus Stories will quickly become a classroom favorite!

CONTENTS

Story 1 – (page 6)
New Words: and, big, little

Directions: Copy the story found on page 6 and the top of this page. Color the pictures and cut them out. Fold the story and read it. Glue each rebus picture in the correct space in the story. Practice reading the story to a friend and then take the story home and read it to your family.

Story 2 – (page 7)
New Words: at, look

Directions: Copy the story found on page 7 and the bottom of this page. Color the pictures and cut them out. Fold the story and read it. Glue each rebus picture in the correct space in the story. Practice reading the story to a friend and then take the story home and read it to your family.

Name

Story 1 – New Words: and, big, little

Big (glue here).

Little (glue here).

1

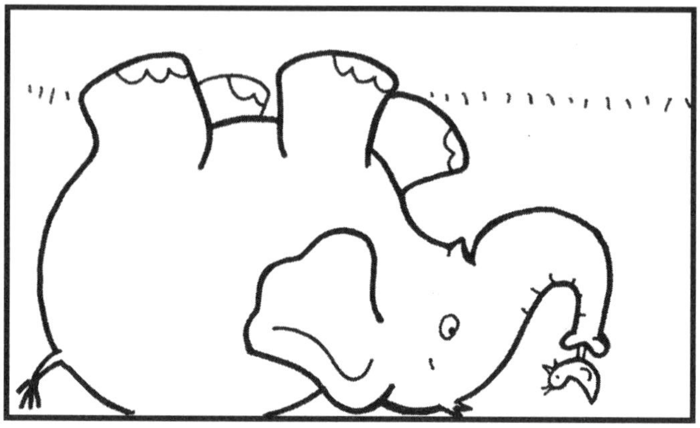

Big (glue here).

Little (glue here).

2

FOLD #1

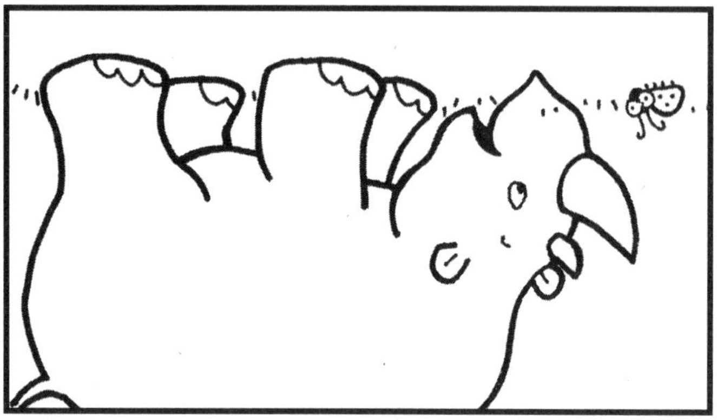

Little (glue here)

and big (glue here).

3

Big (glue here) and

little (glue here).

4

FOLD #2

Story 2 – New Words: at, look

Name ____________

Look at (glue here).

1

Look at (glue here).

2

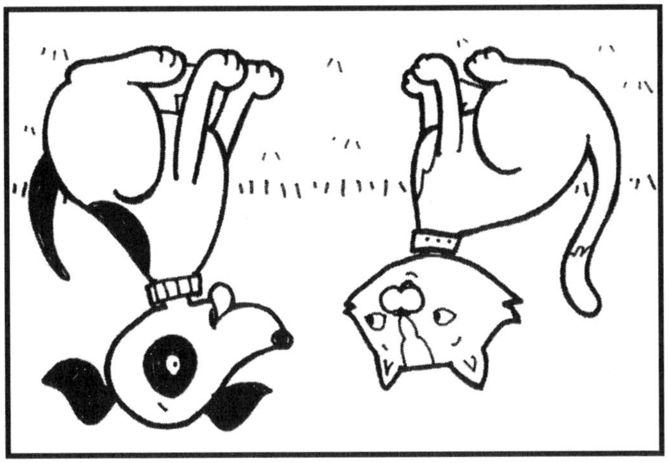

Look at (glue here) and (glue here).

3

FOLD #1

Look!

Look at (glue here) and (glue here)!

4

FOLD #2

 KE-804099 © Key Education • *Cut, Color, Trace & Paste Rebus Stories*

Story 3 – (page 9)
New Words: in, play, the

Directions: Copy the story found on page 9 and the top of this page. Color the pictures and cut them out. Fold the story and read it. Glue each rebus picture in the correct space in the story. Practice reading the story to a friend and then take the story home and read it to your family.

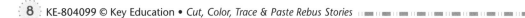

Story 4 – (page 10)
New Words: can, I, you

Directions: Copy the story found on page 10 and the bottom of this page. Color the pictures and cut them out. Fold the story and read it. Glue each rebus picture in the correct space in the story. Practice reading the story to a friend and then take the story home and read it to your family.

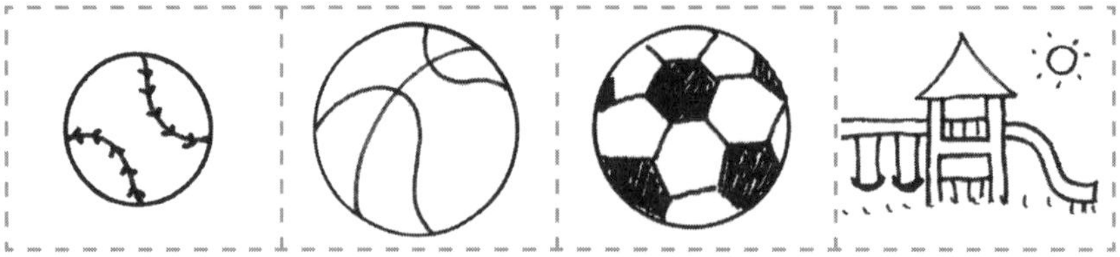

Name

Story 3 – New Words: in, play, the

Look at (glue here)

and (glue here) play.

1

(glue here) plays in

the (glue here).

2

(glue here) plays in

the (glue here).

3

Look at (glue here)

and (glue here) play

in the (glue here).

4

FOLD #1

FOLD #2

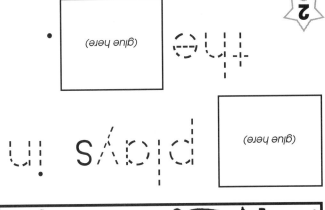

Name

Story 4 – New Words: can, I, you

Look, I can play (glue here).

1

2

You can play (glue here).

3

You and I can play (glue here).

FOLD #1

You and I can play in the (glue here).

4

FOLD #2

KE-804099 © Key Education • *Cut, Color, Trace & Paste Rebus Stories*

Story 5 – (page 12)
New Words: me, see

Directions: Copy the story found on page 12 and the top of this page. Color the pictures and cut them out. Fold the story and read it. Glue each rebus picture in the correct space in the story. Practice reading the story to a friend and then take the story home and read it to your family.

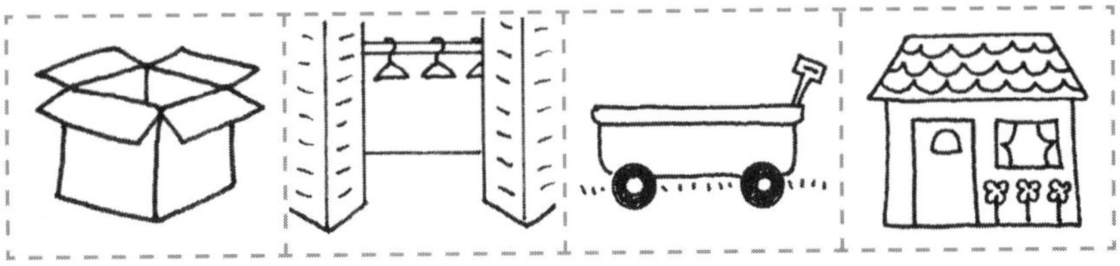

Review Story 6 – (page 13)
New Words: and, at, big, can, I, in, little, look, me, play, see, the, you

Directions: Copy the story found on page 13 and the bottom of this page. Color the pictures and cut them out. Fold the story and read it. Glue each rebus picture in the correct space in the story. Practice reading the story to a friend and then take the story home and read it to your family.

Name

Story 5 – New Words: me, see

Can you see me in the (glue here) .

1

2

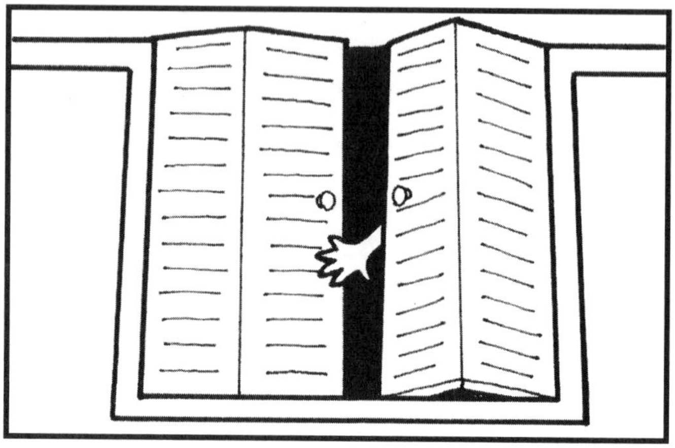

Can you see me in the (glue here) .

3

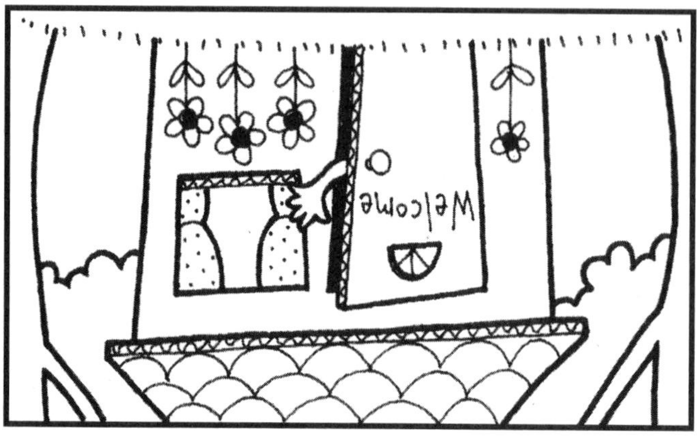

Can you see me in the (glue here) .

FOLD #1

Look! You can see me in the (glue here) .

4

FOLD #2

Review Story 6 – Words from Stories 1–5: and, at, big, can, I, in, little, look, me, play, see, the, you

Name

I see a big (glue here) .

1

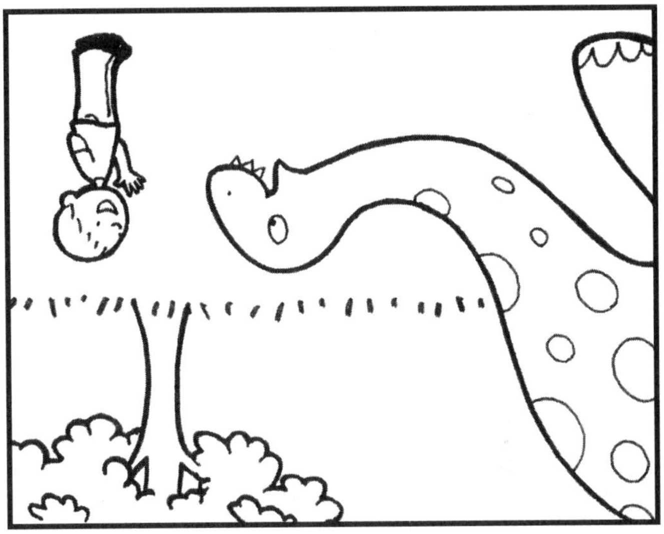

Can the big (glue here) play.

2

Look at me! See me and the big (glue here) play.

3

Big (glue here) and I play and play.

4

FOLD #1

FOLD #2

 KE-804099 © Key Education • *Cut, Color, Trace & Paste Rebus Stories*

Story 7 – (page 15)
New Words: down, go, up

Directions: Copy the story found on page 15 and the top of this page. Color the pictures and cut them out. Fold the story and read it. Glue each rebus picture in the correct space in the story. Practice reading the story to a friend and then take the story home and read it to your family.

Story 8 – (page 16)
New Words: do, like

Directions: Copy the story found on page 16 and the bottom of this page. Color the pictures and cut them out. Fold the story and read it. Glue each rebus picture in the correct space in the story. Practice reading the story to a friend and then take the story home and read it to your family.

14 KE-804099 © Key Education • *Cut, Color, Trace & Paste Rebus Stories*

Name

Story 7 – New Words: down, go, up

Look at (glue here) go up.

1

2

Look at (glue here) go down.

3

(glue here) and (glue here) go up and down.

FOLD #1

Can (glue here) and (glue here) go up and down in the (glue here).

4

FOLD #2

KE-804099 © Key Education • *Cut, Color, Trace & Paste Rebus Stories*

Name

Story 8 – New Words: do, like

Do you like

to (glue here) ?

1

Do you like

to go in

the (glue here) ?

2

Do you like

to play in

the (glue here) ?

3

FOLD #1

Look, I do!

I like me —

a (glue here) !

4

FOLD #2

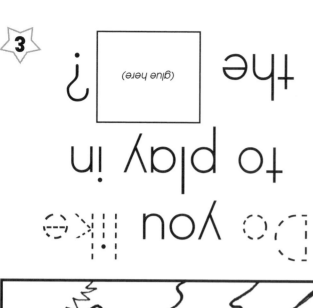

Story 9 – (page 18)
New Word: this

Directions: Copy the story found on page 18 and the top of this page. Color the pictures and cut them out. Fold the story and read it. Glue each rebus picture in the correct space in the story. Practice reading the story to a friend and then take the story home and read it to your family.

Story 10 – (page 19)
New Words: a, have, we

Directions: Copy the story found on page 19 and the bottom of this page. Color the pictures and cut them out. Fold the story and read it. Glue each rebus picture in the correct space in the story. Practice reading the story to a friend and then take the story home and read it to your family.

Name

Story 9 – New Word: this

Can you do this?

I can (glue here) !

1

2

Look! I can do this.

I can (glue here) !

3

Look at me! Can you do this?

I can (glue here) !

FOLD #1

You can do this!

You can (glue here) !

4

FOLD #2

Story 10 – New Words: a, have, we

Name

We have a big (glue here) and a little (glue here).

1

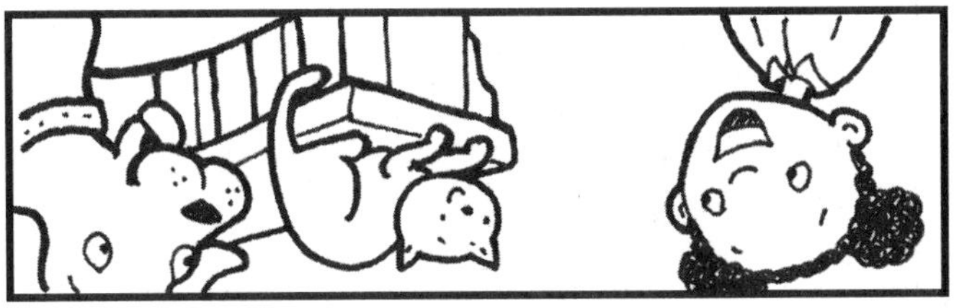

We have to play. Big (glue here) and little (glue here) like to play.

2

We can play in the (glue here).

3

FOLD #1

We have (glue here) play.

Go, big (glue here)!

4

FOLD #2

Story 11 – (page 21)
New Words: is, my

Directions: Copy the story found on page 21 and the top of this page. Color the pictures and cut them out. Fold the story and read it. Glue each rebus picture in the correct space in the story. Practice reading the story to a friend and then take the story home and read it to your family.

Review Story 12 – (page 22)
New Words: a, do, down, go, have, is, like, my, this, up, we

Directions: Copy the story found on page 22 and the bottom of this page. Color the pictures and cut them out. Fold the story and read it. Glue each rebus picture in the correct space in the story. Practice reading the story to a friend and then take the story home and read it to your family.

Name

Story 11 – New Words: is, my

This is my (glue here).

I like my (glue here).

1

This is my (glue here).

I like my (glue here).

2

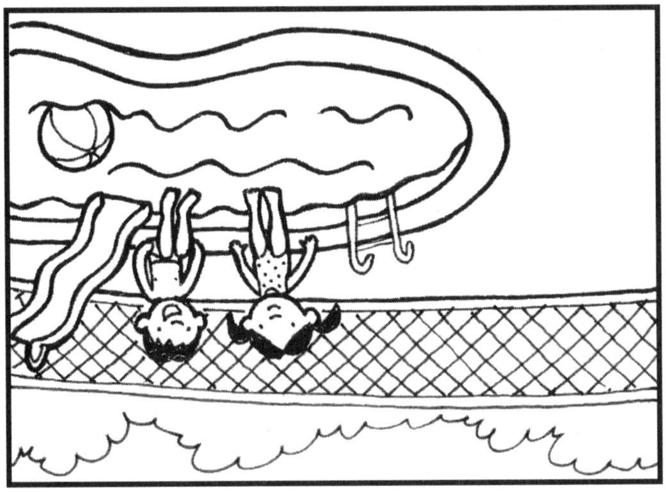

Do you like my (glue here).

3

FOLD #1

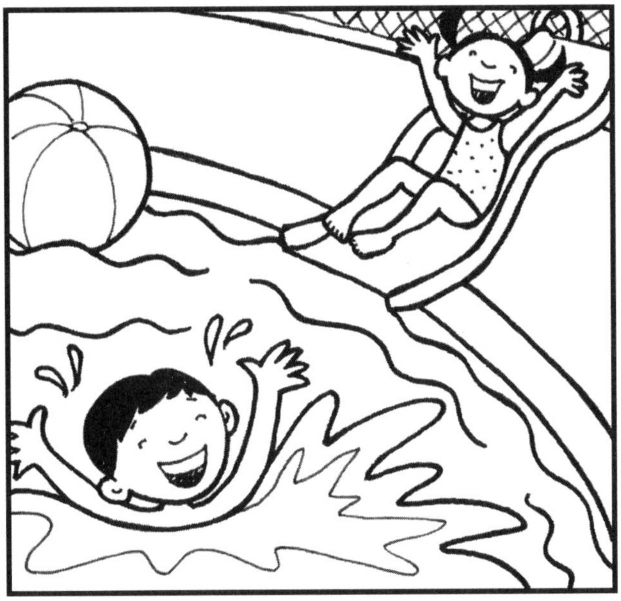

I like this!
I like this!

4

FOLD #2

Name

Review Story 12 – Words from Stories 7–11:
a, do, down, go, have, is, like, my, this, up, we

1

We see this (glue here) !
We like it.

2

Can we go up in the (glue here) ?

3

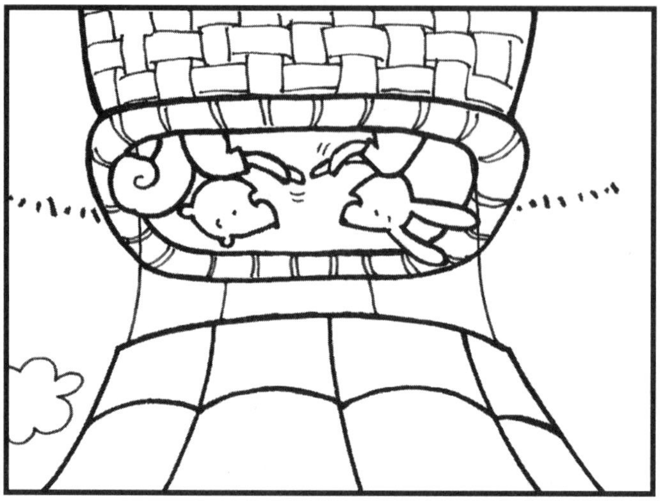

We can play in the (glue here) .

FOLD #1

FOLD #2

4

We can see.
Can the (glue here) go down?

KE-804099 © Key Education • *Cut, Color, Trace & Paste Rebus Stories*

Story 13 – (page 24)
New Words: are, here

Directions: Copy the story found on page 24 and the top of this page. Color the pictures and cut them out. Fold the story and read it. Glue each rebus picture in the correct space in the story. Practice reading the story to a friend and then take the story home and read it to your family.

Story 14 – (page 25)
New Words: funny, it

Directions: Copy the story found on page 25 and the bottom of this page. Color the pictures and cut them out. Fold the story and read it. Glue each rebus picture in the correct space in the story. Practice reading the story to a friend and then take the story home and read it to your family.

Name

Story 13 – New Words: are, here

Here we are!

We are at the (glue here).

1

Here is (glue here).

(glue here) can play here.

2

(glue here) and (glue here) are here.

3

FOLD #1

Are you (glue here) you are here?

4

FOLD #2

KE-804099 © Key Education • Cut, Color, Trace & Paste Rebus Stories

Name

Story 14 – New Words: funny, it

I like it.
It is a
funny (glue here).

1

Do you
like the
funny (glue here).

2

Here it is.
See the
funny (glue here).

3

FOLD #1

FOLD #2

The (glue here) is
funny.
I like it.

4

Story 15 – (page 27)
New Words: he, she

Directions: Copy the story found on page 27 and the top of this page. Color the pictures and cut them out. Fold the story and read it. Glue each rebus picture in the correct space in the story. Practice reading the story to a friend and then take the story home and read it to your family.

Story 16 – (page 28)
New Words: jump, run

Directions: Copy the story found on page 28 and the bottom of this page. Color the pictures and cut them out. Fold the story and read it. Glue each rebus picture in the correct space in the story. Practice reading the story to a friend and then take the story home and read it to your family.

Name

Story 15 – New Words: he, she

She is funny. She is a (glue here).

1

He is funny. He is a (glue here).

2

He and she like to play in the (glue here).

3

FOLD #1

He is not funny in the (glue here).

4

FOLD #2

Name

Story 16 – New Words: jump, run

Look at

(glue here)

jump.

He can

jump up!

1

Look at

(glue here)

run.

She can

run down!

2

He can jump

in the

(glue here)

.

She can run

in the

(glue here)

.

3

(glue here)

and

(glue here)

run and jump

up and down and

up and down.

4

FOLD #1

FOLD #2

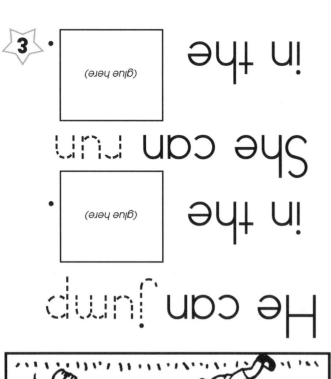

KE-804099 © Key Education • Cut, Color, Trace & Paste Rebus Stories

Story 17 – (page 30)
New Word: they

Directions: Copy the story found on page 30 and the top of this page. Color the pictures and cut them out. Fold the story and read it. Glue each rebus picture in the correct space in the story. Practice reading the story to a friend and then take the story home and read it to your family.

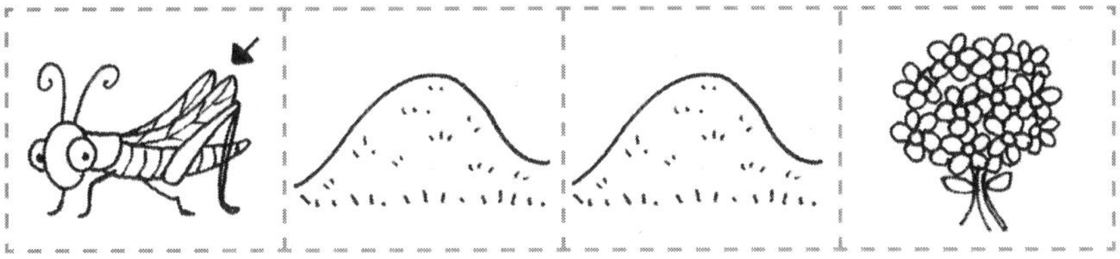

Review Story 18 – (page 31)
New Words: are, funny, he, here, it, jump, run, she, they

Directions: Copy the story found on page 31 and the bottom of this page. Color the pictures and cut them out. Fold the story and read it. Glue each rebus picture in the correct space in the story. Practice reading the story to a friend and then take the story home and read it to your family.

KE-804099 © Key Education • *Cut, Color, Trace & Paste Rebus Stories* 29

Name

Story 17 – New Word: they

They like to play. They play (glue here).

1

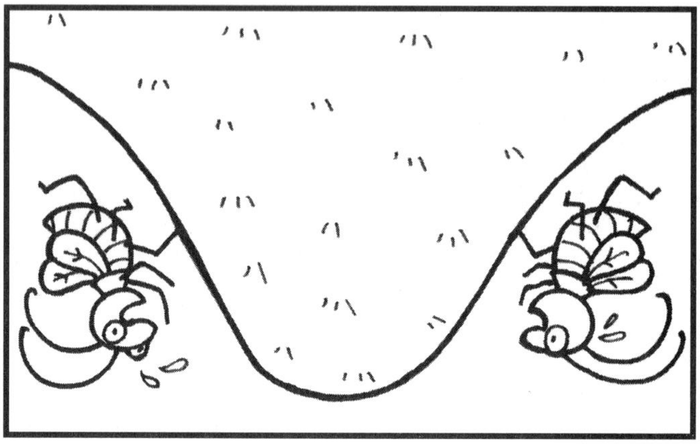

They like to run. They run up the (glue here).

2

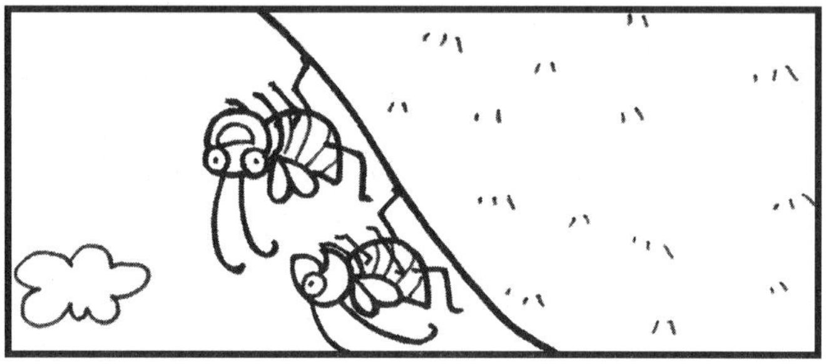

They like to jump. They jump down the (glue here).

3

FOLD #1

They like to play and run and jump in the (glue here).

4

FOLD #2

Name

Review Story 18 – Words from Stories 13–17:
are, funny, he, here, it, jump, run, she, they

I have

a little (glue here).

She is funny.

1

FOLD #2

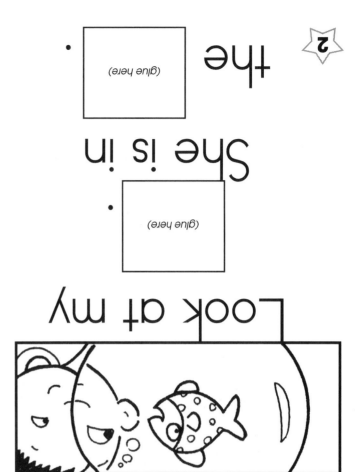

Look at my (glue here).

She is in

the (glue here).

2

You can see

my (glue here).

She can (glue here).

3

FOLD #1

We can look

at my (glue here).

She can look

at (glue here).

4

KE-804099 © Key Education • Cut, Color, Trace & Paste Rebus Stories

Story 19 – (page 33)
New Words: come, to

Directions: Copy the story found on page 33 and the top of this page. Color the pictures and cut them out. Fold the story and read it. Glue each rebus picture in the correct space in the story. Practice reading the story to a friend and then take the story home and read it to your family.

Story 20 – (page 34)
New Words: get, good

Directions: Copy the story found on page 34 and the bottom of this page. Color the pictures and cut them out. Fold the story and read it. Glue each rebus picture in the correct space in the story. Practice reading the story to a friend and then take the story home and read it to your family.

Name

Story 19 – New Words: come, to

Come to my (glue here) to play. We can have fun.

1

Come! Run to the (glue here)!

2

Come! We can jump in the (glue here).

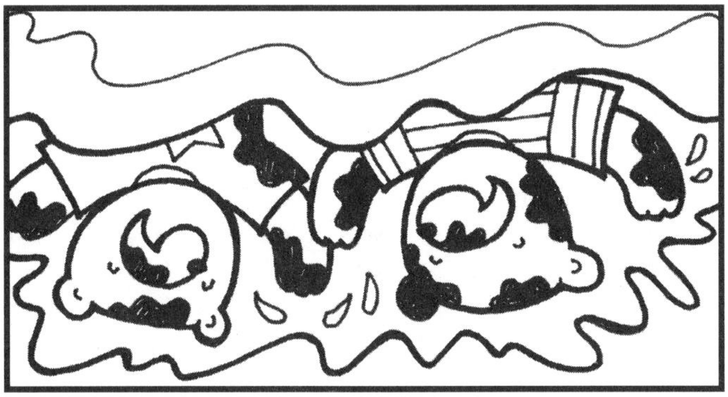

3

FOLD #1

Come to me! You are (glue here). Come and (glue here).

4

FOLD #2

Story 20 – New Words: get, good

Name

I get to ride you. You are a good (glue here) !

1

2

I can get you. Good (glue here) !

3

Get down (glue here) .

Good (glue here) !

Come here!

FOLD #1

4

Good!

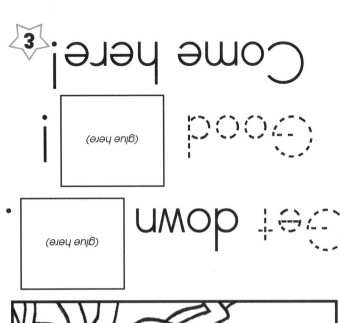

I get to ride the (glue here) !

FOLD #2

KE-804099 © Key Education • Cut, Color, Trace & Paste Rebus Stories

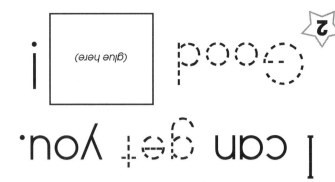

Story 21 – (page 36)
New Words: help, not

Directions: Copy the story found on page 36 and the top of this page. Color the pictures and cut them out. Fold the story and read it. Glue each rebus picture in the correct space in the story. Practice reading the story to a friend and then take the story home and read it to your family.

Story 22 – (page 37)
New Words: for, on

Directions: Copy the story found on page 37 and the bottom of this page. Color the pictures and cut them out. Fold the story and read it. Glue each rebus picture in the correct space in the story. Practice reading the story to a friend and then take the story home and read it to your family.

KE-804099 © Key Education • *Cut, Color, Trace & Paste Rebus Stories* 35

Name

Story 21 – New Words: help, not

Help me!
Look up at
the (glue here).
This is not good.

1

2

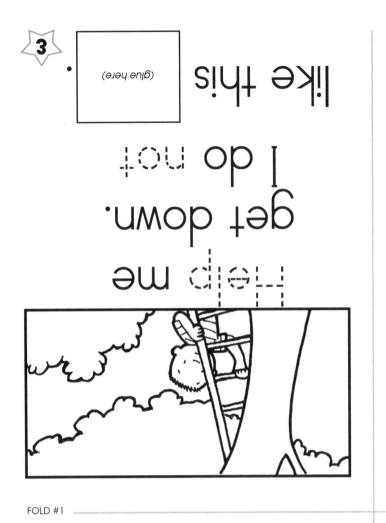

Help!
Look up at
the (glue here).
I cannot get
down.

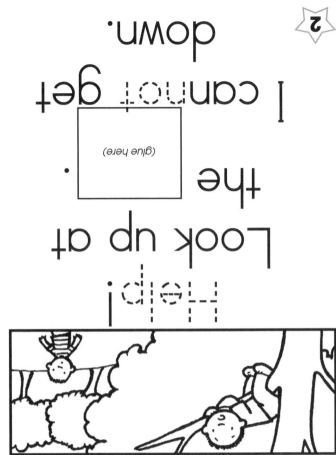

3

Help me
get down.
I do not
like this (glue here).

FOLD #1

This is not help!
This is not good!
We are (glue here).

4

FOLD #2

Name

Story 22 – New Words: for, on

This (glue here) is for you.

Get on it!

1

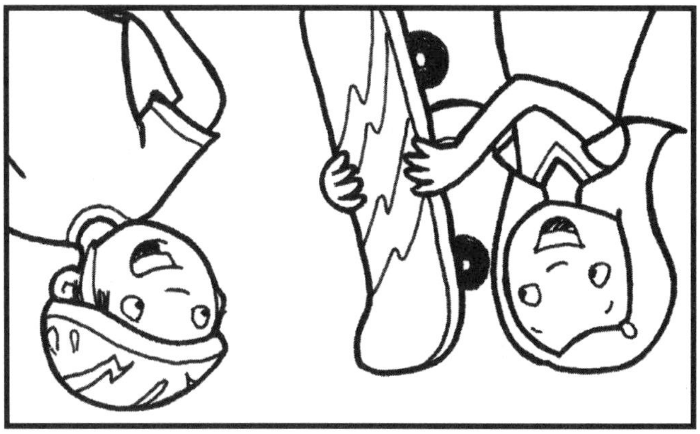

This (glue here) is for you.

Get on it!

2

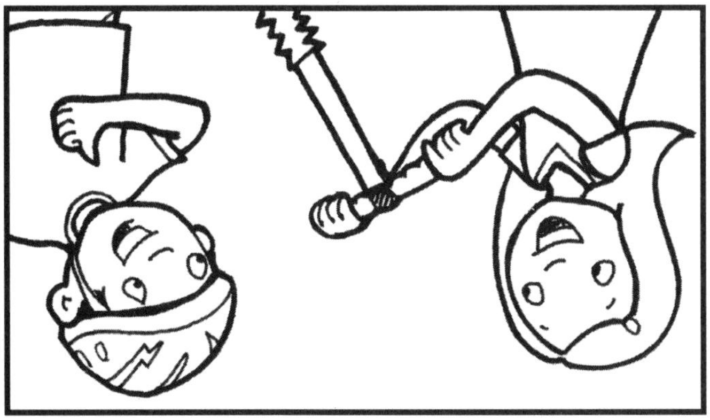

This (glue here) is for you.

Get on it!

3

FOLD #1

This (glue here) is for you.

Do not get on it!

4

FOLD #2

Story 23 – (page 39)
New Word: find

Directions: Copy the story found on page 39 and the top of this page. Color the pictures and cut them out. Fold the story and read it. Glue each rebus picture in the correct space in the story. Practice reading the story to a friend and then take the story home and read it to your family.

Review Story 24 – (page 40)
New Words: come, find, for, get, good, help, not, on, to

Directions: Copy the story found on page 40 and the bottom of this page. Color the pictures and cut them out. Fold the story and read it. Glue each rebus picture in the correct space in the story. Practice reading the story to a friend and then take the story home and read it to your family.

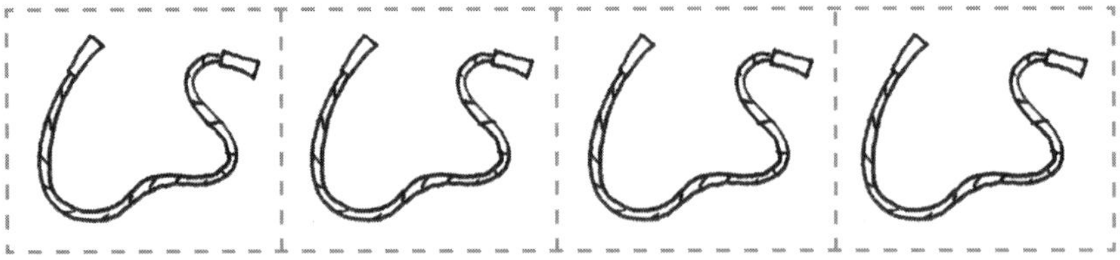

Story 23 – New Word: find

Name

Come find me!
Look in the (glue here).

1

Can you
find me?
Look here,
in the (glue here).

2

find me!
Look up in
the (glue here).

3

Good! You can
find me!
I like it up
in the (glue here).

4

FOLD #1

FOLD #2

KE-804099 © Key Education • Cut, Color, Trace & Paste Rebus Stories

Name

Review Story 24 – Words from Stories 19–23:
come, find, for, get, good, help, not, on, to

Do not help

me jump (glue here).

1

2

I can jump (glue here).

Do not help me!

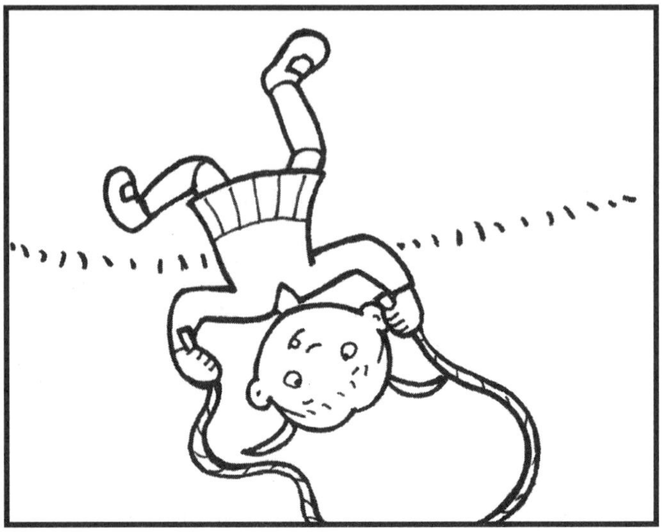

3

Down! Down!

funny jump (glue here).

This is not a

FOLD #1

Look at me!

I can

jump (glue here).

4

FOLD #2

KE-804099 © Key Education • *Cut, Color, Trace & Paste Rebus Stories*

Story 25 – (page 42)
New Words: but, said

Directions: Copy the story found on page 42 and the top of this page. Color the pictures and cut them out. Fold the story and read it. Glue each rebus picture in the correct space in the story. Practice reading the story to a friend and then take the story home and read it to your family.

Story 26 – (page 43)
New Words: did, make

Directions: Copy the story found on page 43 and the bottom of this page. Color the pictures and cut them out. Fold the story and read it. Glue each rebus picture in the correct space in the story. Practice reading the story to a friend and then take the story home and read it to your family.

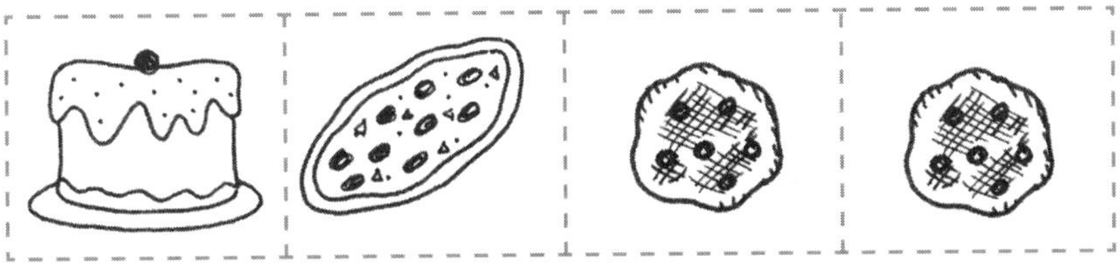

Name

Story 25: New Words: but, said

She said, "I like you. Here are (glue here)."

1

2

He said, "I do not like (glue here)."

3

She said, "I do not like you, but I like (glue here)."

FOLD #1

He said, "I do not like (glue here), but I like you!

4

FOLD #2

KE-804099 © Key Education • *Cut, Color, Trace & Paste Rebus Stories*

Story 26 – New Words: did, make

Name

Did you make this (glue here) ?

She said, "I did."

1

2

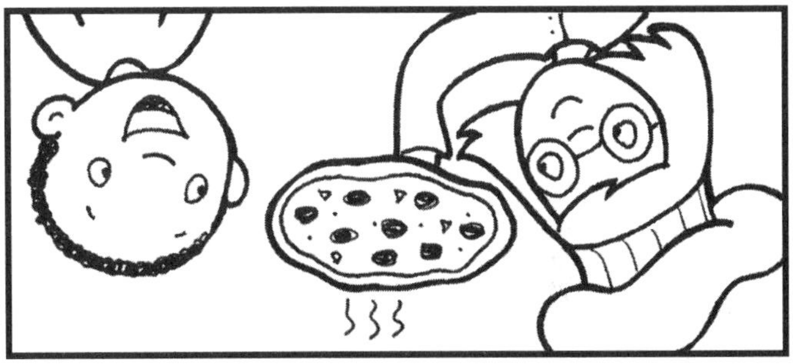

Did you make this (glue here) ?

She said, "I did."

3

Did you make this (glue here) ?

She said, "I did."

FOLD #1

She said, "Did you like the (glue here) ?"

He said, "I did not."

4

FOLD #2

Story 27 – (page 45)
New Words: pretty, so

Directions: Copy the story found on page 45 and the top of this page. Color the pictures and cut them out. Fold the story and read it. Glue each rebus picture in the correct space in the story. Practice reading the story to a friend and then take the story home and read it to your family.

Story 28 – (page 46)
New Words: eat, want

Directions: Copy the story found on page 46 and the bottom of this page. Color the pictures and cut them out. Fold the story and read it. Glue each rebus picture in the correct space in the story. Practice reading the story to a friend and then take the story home and read it to your family.

44 KE-804099 © Key Education • *Cut, Color, Trace & Paste Rebus Stories*

Story 27 – New Words: pretty, so

Name

Go find the pretty (glue here).

She is so pretty.

1

2

I have a (glue here).

So, can you get the pretty (glue here)?

3

Run! Run!

The pretty (glue here) can go up!

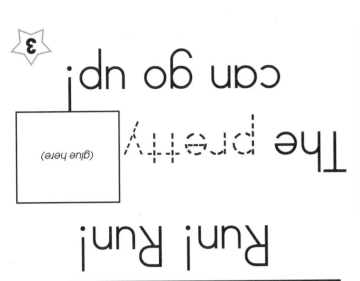

FOLD #1

She is so pretty.

And you look so funny!

4

FOLD #2

Name

Story 28 – New Words: eat, want

Do you want
to eat
a (glue here)?

1

I can make you
a (glue here) to eat.

2

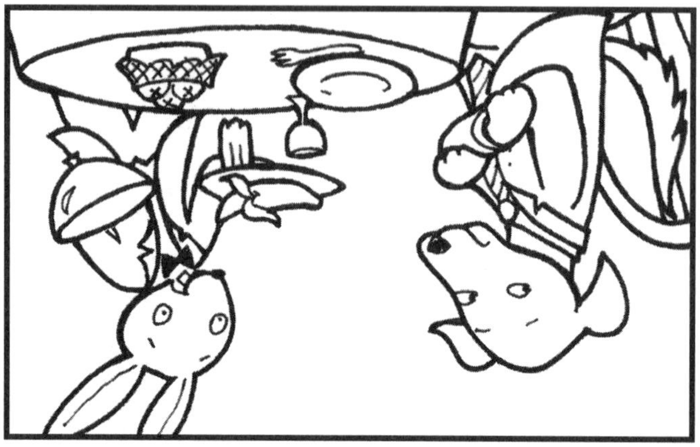

Do you want
to eat?
Eat a (glue here)?

3

So, you want
to eat!

Have a (glue here)?

4

FOLD #1

FOLD #2

Story 29 – (page 48)
New Words: blue, red, yellow

Directions: Copy the story found on page 48 and the top of this page. Color the pictures and cut them out. Fold the story and read it. Glue each rebus picture in the correct space in the story. Practice reading the story to a friend and then take the story home and read it to your family.

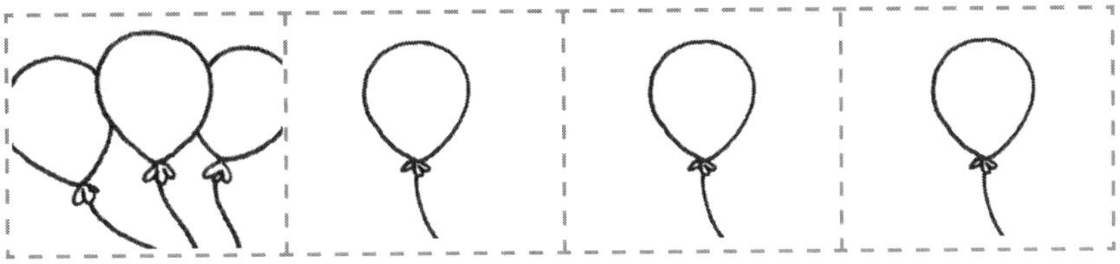

Review Story 30 – (page 49)
New Words: blue, did, eat, make, pretty, red, said, so, want, yellow

Directions: Copy the story found on page 49 and the bottom of this page. Color the pictures and cut them out. Fold the story and read it. Glue each rebus picture in the correct space in the story. Practice reading the story to a friend and then take the story home and read it to your family.

Name

Story 29 – New Words: blue, red, yellow

Jump on!
I want to get
red, blue, and
yellow (glue here).

1

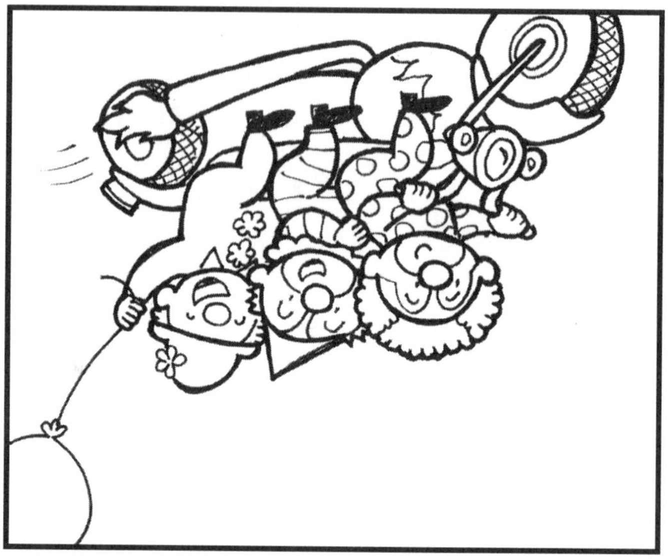

You can have
a red (glue here).

2

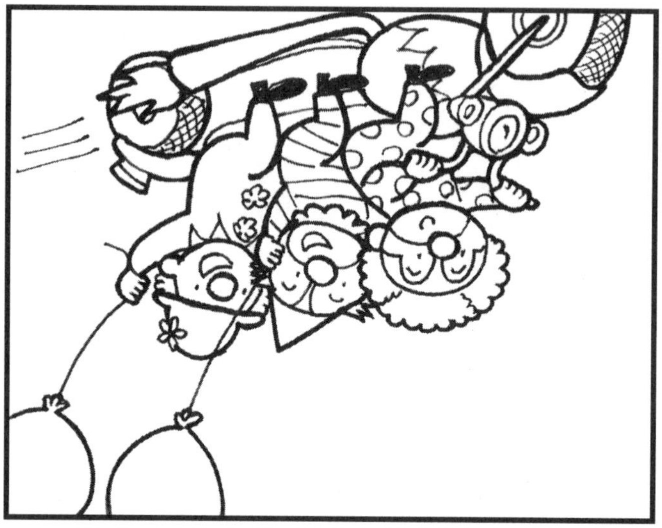

You can have
a blue (glue here).

3

FOLD #1

I can have
a yellow (glue here).
Up we go!

4

FOLD #2

Name

Review Story 30 – Words from Stories 25–29:
blue, did, eat, make, pretty, red, said, so, want, yellow

Did you see the pretty red (glue here)?

1

I want to eat the pretty red (glue here).

2

He said, "You cannot eat it. It is my (glue here)."

3

FOLD #1

Look! I see a (glue here) in the (glue here). It is a (glue here) (glue here).

4

FOLD #2

KE-804099 © Key Education • *Cut, Color, Trace & Paste Rebus Stories*

Story 31 – (page 51)
New Words: away, with

Directions: Copy the story found on page 51 and the top of this page. Color the pictures and cut them out. Fold the story and read it. Glue each rebus picture in the correct space in the story. Practice reading the story to a friend and then take the story home and read it to your family.

Story 32 – (page 52)
New Words: be, will

Directions: Copy the story found on page 52 and the bottom of this page. Color the pictures and cut them out. Fold the story and read it. Glue each rebus picture in the correct space in the story. Practice reading the story to a friend and then take the story home and read it to your family.

Name

Story 31 – New Words: away, with

Away with you

(glue here)

. Do not

(glue here)

me.

1

Go away!

Go with this

(glue here)

yellow

2

I want to eat

(glue here)

.

Not with you!

3

FOLD #1

Help! I can run away!

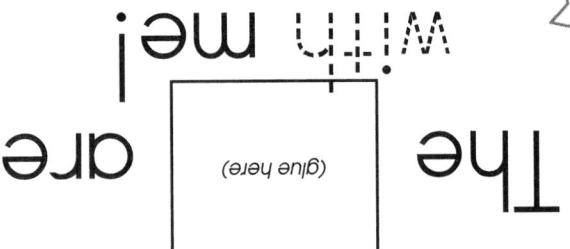

The (glue here) are with me!

4

FOLD #2

KE-804099 © Key Education • *Cut, Color, Trace & Paste Rebus Stories*

Name

Story 32 – New Words: be, will

I like you.

Will you be

my (glue here) ?

1

2

Will you run

with me to

the (glue here) ?

3

Will you jump

with me on

the (glue here) ?

FOLD #1

Will you run

and jump

with me?

Will you be

my (glue here) ?

4

FOLD #2

KE-804099 © Key Education • *Cut, Color, Trace & Paste Rebus Stories*

Story 33 – (page 54)
New Words: one, three, two

Directions: Copy the story found on page 54 and the top of this page. Color the pictures and cut them out. Fold the story and read it. Glue each rebus picture in the correct space in the story. Practice reading the story to a friend and then take the story home and read it to your family.

Story 34 – (page 55)
New Words: know, what

Directions: Copy the story found on page 55 and the bottom of this page. Color the pictures and cut them out. Fold the story and read it. Glue each rebus picture in the correct space in the story. Practice reading the story to a friend and then take the story home and read it to your family.

Name

Story 33 – New Words: one, three, two

One, two, three! I see one (glue here).

1

2

One, two, three! I see two (glue here).

3

One, two, three! I see three (glue here).

FOLD #1

One, two, three! We see three (glue here).

4

FOLD #2

KE-804099 © Key Education • *Cut, Color, Trace & Paste Rebus Stories*

Name

Story 34 – New Words: know, what

What do you want to do? Do you not know?

Play (glue here) ?

1

What do you want to do? Do you not know?

Play with (glue here) ?

2

What do you want to do? Do you not know?

Play with (glue here) ?

3

FOLD #1

I know what we can do! We can play (glue here) and (glue here) and (glue here).

4

FOLD #2

Story 35 – (page 57)
New Words: all, new

Directions: Copy the story found on page 57 and the top of this page. Color the pictures and cut them out. Fold the story and read it. Glue each rebus picture in the correct space in the story. Practice reading the story to a friend and then take the story home and read it to your family.

Review Story 36 – (page 58)
New Words: all, away, be, know, new, one, three, two, what, will, with

Directions: Copy the story found on page 58 and the bottom of this page. Color the pictures and cut them out. Fold the story and read it. Glue each rebus picture in the correct space in the story. Practice reading the story to a friend and then take the story home and read it to your family.

56 KE-804099 © Key Education • *Cut, Color, Trace & Paste Rebus Stories*

Story 35 – New Words: all, new

Name

Look at my (glue here) new.

They are all new!

1

2

Look at my (glue here) new.

They are all new!

3

Look at my (glue here) new.

They are all new!

FOLD #1

All new!

I want a new (glue here).

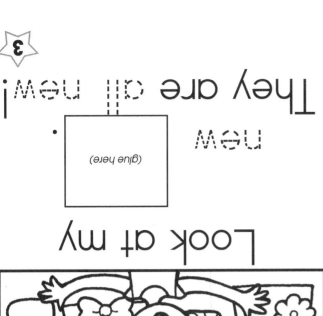

4

FOLD #2

 KE-804095 © Key Education • Cut, Color, Trace & Paste Rebus Stories

Name

Review Story 36 – Words from Stories 31–35:
all, away, be, know, new, one, three, two, what, will, with

Look here!
I see one, two,
and three (glue here) .

1

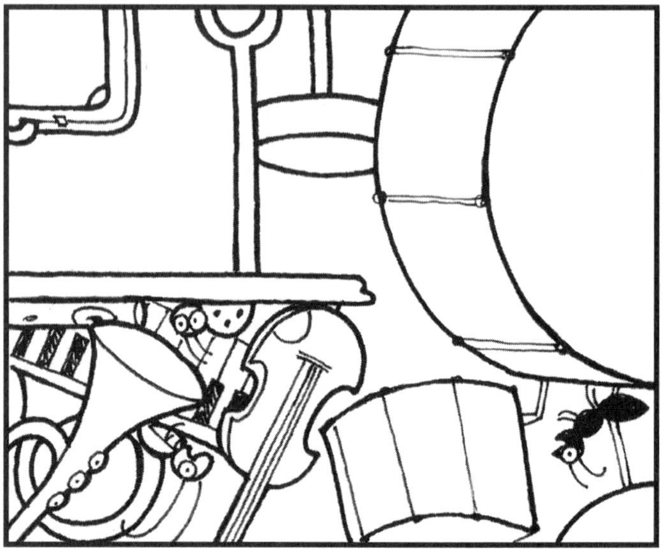

The new (glue here) will be fun to play.

2

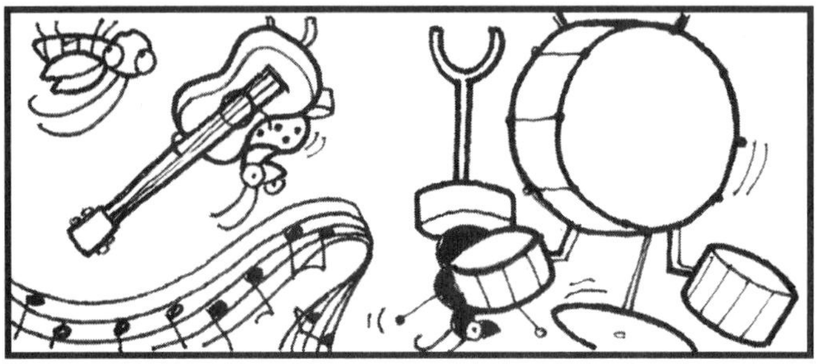

I know I can
the (glue here) .
You can play
the (glue here) .

3

FOLD #1

And, you can
play (glue here) .
We are all good!

4

FOLD #2

KE-804099 © Key Education • *Cut, Color, Trace & Paste Rebus Stories*

Review Story 37 – (page 60)
Review all words

Directions: Copy the story found on page 60 and the top of this page. Color the pictures and cut them out. Fold the story and read it. Glue each rebus picture in the correct space in the story. Practice reading the story to a friend and then take the story home and read it to your family.

Review Story 38 – (page 61)
Review all words

Directions: Copy the story found on page 61 and the bottom of this page. Color the pictures and cut them out. Fold the story and read it. Glue each rebus picture in the correct space in the story. Practice reading the story to a friend and then take the story home and read it to your family.

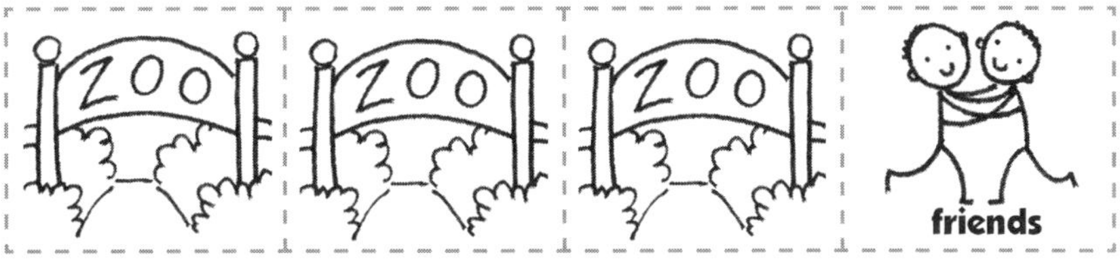

KE-804099 © Key Education • *Cut, Color, Trace & Paste Rebus Stories* 59

Name

Story 37 – Review all words

Will you come

to my (glue here)?

We can play

on my (glue here).

1

We will have fun.

We can eat (glue here)

and look at (glue here).

2

You can (glue here)

at my (glue here)?

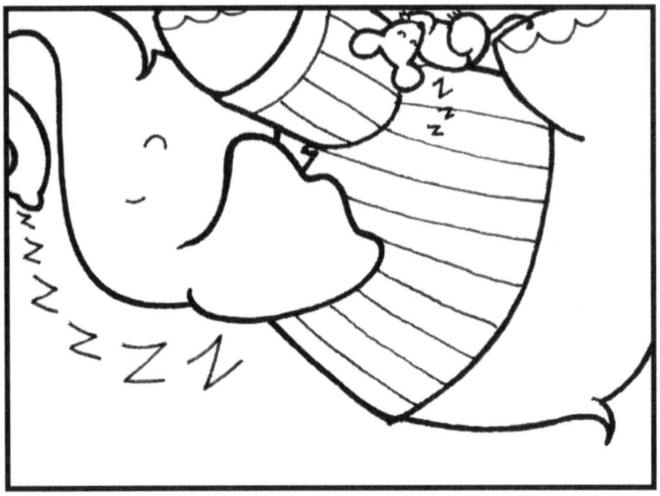

3

FOLD #1

I like you.

You like me.

We are (glue here).

4

FOLD #2

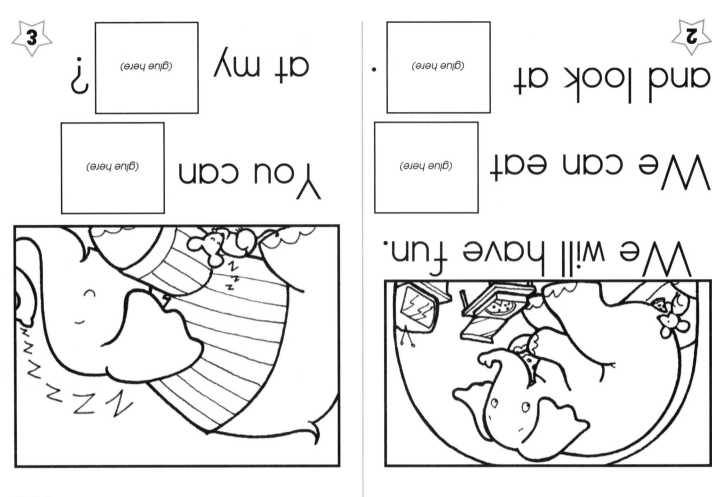

KE-804099 © Key Education • *Cut, Color, Trace & Paste Rebus Stories*

Story 38 – Review all words

Name

She said, "Do you want to go to the (glue here)?"

1

He said, "I will go. I like the (glue here)."

2

She said, "What will we see at the (glue here)?"

3

FOLD #1

He said, "We will see my (glue here)."

4

FOLD #2

KE-804099 © Key Education • *Cut, Color, Trace & Paste Rebus Stories*

3

2

FOLD #1

My Own Story

Title:____

____

Written by:____________________________________

FOLD #2

4

1

Word List

a
all
and
are
at
away
be
big
blue
can
come
did
do
down
eat
find

for
funny
get
go
good
have
he
help
here
I
in
is
it
jump
know
like

little
look
make
me
my
new
not
on
one
play
pretty
red
run
said
see
she

so
the
they
this
three
to
two
up
want
we
what
will
with
yellow
you

Correlations to the Standards

This book supports the NCTE/IRA *Standards for the English Language Arts* and the recommended teaching practices outlined in the NAEYC/IRA position statement *Learning to Read and Write: Developmentally Appropriate Practices for Young Children.*

NCTE/IRA Standards for the English Language Arts

Each activity in this book supports one or more of the following standards:

1. **Students read many different types of print and nonprint texts for a variety of purposes.** Students read thirty-eight different rebus stories that incorporate both words and pictures in this book.

2. **Students use a variety of strategies to build meaning while reading.** *Cut, Color, Trace, & Paste Rebus Stories* reinforces sight word recognition and vocabulary skills that are essential to effective reading.

3. **Students communicate in spoken, written, and visual form, for a variety of purposes and a variety of audiences.** Students speak while reading aloud, write while tracing words and writing their own stories, and communicate visually by coloring, cutting, and pasting while doing the activities in this book.

NAEYC/IRA Position Statement
Learning to Read and Write: Developmentally Appropriate Practices for Young Children

The activities in this book support the following recommended teaching practices for Kindergarten and Primary students:

1. **Teachers read to children daily and provide opportunities for students to independently read both fiction and nonfiction texts.** Students read the stories in Rebus Stories aloud to their friends and families.

2. **Teachers provide opportunities for students to write many different kinds of texts for different purposes.** Students trace words and write their own stories in *Cut, Color, Trace, & Paste Rebus Stories.*

3. **Teachers provide challenging instruction that expands children's knowledge of their world and expands vocabulary.** *Cut, Color, Trace, & Paste Rebus Stories* helps expand students' vocabularies by reinforcing 50 sight words and additional story-specific vocabulary.